The Art of

CHINESE COOKING

by

the Benedictine Sisters

of Peking

Illustrations by M. Kuwata

CHARLES E. TUTTLE COMPANY

Rutland, Vermont   Tokyo, Japan

Published by the Charles E. Tuttle Company
of Rutland, Vermont & Tokyo, Japan with
editorial offices at 15 Edogawa-cho,
Bunkyo-ku, Tokyo

Library of Congress Catalog Card No. 56-11125

First edition, June, 1956
Third printing, October, 1956

Printed in Japan by
Obun Printing Company, Ltd.

FOREWORD

Lessons in Chinese cookery in Tokyo conducted by American nuns may seem a little farfetched, but there's good reason for it. When Sister Regia and I first went to China in 1930 as missionaries at the Catholic University of Peking and later in Kaifeng, Honan Province, we learned to enjoy the tastiness and infinite variety of Chinese cooking. Of course we had to—Western-style cooking wasn't generally available. When Ta Shih Fu, our cook, would prepare a meal, we were right at his heels, watching everything he did and sometimes stopping him in mid-swing to measure exactly how much soy sauce or how many bamboo shoots he put into the dish. Little did we know that our interest would some day provide our daily bread and (sometimes) a little butter !

Suddenly World War II was upon us, and within two hours after the attack on Pearl Harbor the Japanese army (already in Kaifeng) had rounded us up in a civilian concentration camp for the duration. Fancy cooking was out, but we could always dream about Chinese food. After the war we returned to Kaifeng and enjoyed once more our favorite dishes. Then came the Communists, pushing us from Kaifeng to Shanghai and finally to Formosa. In 1950 the American Consul thought Formosa might become too dangerous, so we shipped off once more, joined by Sister M. Ursuline, who had been with us in China since 1936. This time we came to Japan. In Tokyo we had literally nothing, but with the kindness of the Very Reverend Hildebrand Yaiser, O.S.B. and the encouragement of Hazel Zimmerman, Marie Richards, and Agatha Jones we thought we might eke out an existence by teaching our friends in Japan what we had learned from Ta Shih Fu. This was a natural decision, since Sister Regia had always been interested in cooking and I had received an M.S. in Home Economics from the University of Minnesota in 1926 and taught home economics in high school and college in the United States for fifteen years before going to China. Our school has grown by leaps and bounds from six students a week to 150 a week.

We want to express our unbounded gratitude to those first few students who stood by loyally, even when many times they didn't get enough to eat. Without them our school would never have developed. And we want to thank Helen S. Agoa for helping us prepare this book.

Our recipes, most of which we use in our school, have been selected with the availability of ingredients in mind, and you should be able to prepare them in any part of the Western world. They are chiefly from northern China and are the type used in good Chinese homes, not necessarily in restaurants. Good luck with them!

Tokyo, Japan   Sister M. Francetta, O.S.B.
March 1956

TABLE OF CONTENTS

TRICKS OF THE TRADE

Aji-no-Moto. Aji-no-Moto (Japanese), Vetsin (Chinese), Accent, and Gourmet Power are trade names for monosodium glutamate. It is a white powder used in bringing out the flavors of foods.

Bamboo Shoots. Bamboo shoots are available in cans. Remove from can, rinse in cold water, and scrape out the white calcium deposit sometimes found in the center of the shoots.

Bean Sprouts. Use fresh ones whenever available. 3 C. fresh bean sprouts, uncooked, equal one-half pound. 1 1/2 C. cooked bean sprouts equal one-half pound.

Coolie Hat Pan. The Chinese cooking pan, shaped like a coolie hat, is extremely useful for all these recipes, both for deep-oil frying and general cooking. Aluminum makes the best pan, being easy to keep clean and yet heating rapidly. Stainless steel cleans easily but food tends to sick in it slightly. Ordinary iron pans are not suitable because they rust. These pans, when made of aluminum or stainless steel, are good for storing partly cooked food.

Cream. 1 C. unwhipped cream makes 2 C. whipped cream.

Flour. Sift all flour before using it in these recipes.

Ginger. Fresh ginger root is best. Plant a root in your garden or in a flower pot and dig up a small piece when needed. Wash it and scrape or peel it before using. Ginger should be used as directed; for instance, it must never be grated except in a minute amount. If fresh ginger is not available, 1/8 t. ground ginger is equivalent to 1 T. of fresh chopped ginger. Ginger may be omitted from any of these recipes.

Grams. The sizes of cans are given in ounces, except for foreign canned foods, when grams are used. One ounce equals 28 grams.

Measurements. Measure chopped ingredients **after** chopping. Abbreviations: T. = tablespoon; t. = teaspoon; C. = cup.

Mushrooms. Dried mushrooms have an excellent flavor. To use them, rinse well, cover them with lukewarm water, and let stand 15 to 20 minutes, until they are spongy. Squeeze them out and save the water. Take off stems, as they are tougher and need longer cooking. If dried mushrooms are not available, use canned ones. One 3 oz. can is equivalent to 6 dried mushrooms. The juice from canned mushrooms may be salty, so this should be taken into account in using it.

Oil. Frying in oil (any vegetable oil) is handy and the results are digestible. In all instances except in frying onions and in deep-fat frying, heat the pan first, add oil, and immediately add the food to be fried. For onions and deep-fat frying, heat the pan and oil first.

Reading Recipes. Before starting to cook, read each recipe three times!

Servings. The servings mentioned in these recipes are small, on the assumption that several different dishes are to be served, as is usual at a Chinese dinner.

If only one dish is prepared, the servings will be larger and fewer, e. g. Beef and Onions, serving four in this book, will be enough for only two people. All of the dishes are to be served with rice, boiled noodles, or fried noodles.

Soup Stock. Good soup stock is necessary in the preparation of Chinese food. Make it from bones, meat scraps, or scrapings from the bottom of the frying pan after cooking meat, and keep it on hand in the refrigerator. Or make it from bouillon cubes (very salty) or 1/2 t. Aji-no-Moto powder and 1 C. water.

Soy Sauce. This is as important in Chinese cookery as salt in American cookery. It adds distinctive flavor to food and makes of an unpalatable dish one fit for a king. Soy sauce, though salty, is not entirely interchangeable with salt. In these recipes soy sauce means either the Japanese *shoyu* or the Chinese *chiang yu*. None of the American soy sauces should be used in the same amounts. If you cannot get the Japanese or Chinese variety, we caution you to use the American variety very carefully and to taste frequently to judge the correct amount. Use only a few drops; it is very salty and much more concentrated than the Oriental brands.

Texture. Chinese dishes are a subtle combination of various consistencies, from the creaminess of bean curd to the crispness of water chestnuts. Hence our watchword : **Do not overcook the vegetables. They should be "crunchy."**

Water Chestnuts. They are now available in cans, but they are expensive. They may be omitted from these recipes, or the amount may be cut down.

Pork

BRAISED PORK WITH OR WITHOUT BEAN CURD

P'eng Chu Jou Tou Fu 烹豚肉豆腐

Make a stock of **3 C. hot water, 2 bouillon cubes,** and **1/2 t. Aji-no-Moto** powder or Accent (monosodium glutamate). Place **2 lbs. pork** cut in 1-inch pieces in kettle and pour over it stock, **1/2 C. soy sauce, 3 T. sherry, 3 C. onions,** sliced lengthwise, **1/3 C. fresh ginger,** thinly shredded, **2 cloves garlic,** minced, and **2 T. brown sugar.** Bring to a boil. Do not cover. Simmer one half hour or until pork is tender. Add **1 T. cornstarch** mixed with **1/4 C. cold water.** Simmer until smooth and thickened, stirring constantly.

If bean curd is used, simmer for 20 minutes **2 cakes of bean curd,** each 4 inches by 1 inch. Drain and cut each cake into three pieces and submerge the bean curd in the boiling pork before cornstarch is added. Simmer another half hour and add cornstarch mixture, as above. Serve hot with rice or noodles. Serves 6.

CHOW MEIN

Ch'ao Mien 炒麵

Slice into fine strips, keeping each separate: **2 C. onions** (slice lengthwise), **3 C. celery, 1 can bamboo shoots** (500 grams), drained, and **1 lb. pork,** beef, shrimp, or chicken. In **1 T. oil** fry meat until done. Take from fire. In another pan, slightly saute the onions in **1 T. oil** and add them to the meat. Sauté the bamboo shoots and **3/4 C. mushrooms,** canned or fresh, in **1 T. oil** and add to the meat. Slightly sauté the celery in **1 T. oil** and add to the meat.

Finally add **1 can bean sprouts** (1 lb.), drained or 3 C. fresh bean sprouts, sautéed, **1 T. fresh ginger,** chopped,* and a mixture of **1 t. sugar, 3 T. cornstarch, 5 T. soy sauce,** and **3/4 C. soup stock.** Heat thoroughly, stirring slowly. Serve hot with boiled noodles, fried noodles, or rice. Serves 8 to 10.

Note: Vegetables should be "crunchy."

* To prepare in advance, place sautéed vegetables, bean sprouts, ginger, and meat in separate piles and place in refrigerator. Before serving, reheat meat, gradually mix in the vegetables, and add the mixture of sugar, cornstarch, soy sauce, and soup stock.

LION'S HEAD

Shih Tz'u T'ou 獅子頭

Mix thoroughly **1 lb. uncooked lean pork**, ground, **8 dried mushrooms**, chopped fine, **12 water chestnuts**, chopped fine, **1 C. onions**, chopped, **1 T. fresh ginger**, chopped, **1 egg**, beaten, **1 t. sherry**, **4 T. soy sauce**, **1/2 t. salt**, **2 t. sugar**, **2 t. cornstarch**, and **1 T. oil.** Shape into three large balls or several small ones. Fry balls until brown; drain.

Arrange **1 head cabbage** or 1 head Chinese cabbage, sliced, in a kettle and place the meat balls on it. Add **1 1/2 C. hot water.** Simmer one half hour. Serves 6 to 8.

Note: To reduce odor of cooking cabbage, place several slices of bread on top of the meat balls.

LOTUS ROOT SANDWICH

Lien Ou Jou Mien Pao 蕅夾肉麵包

Heat pan ; add **1 T. oil.** Fry until well done **2 C. ground pork** and **2 C. onion,** chopped. Add **1 T. fresh ginger,** chopped, **2 T. soy sauce,** and **1 T. cornstarch.** Mix well.

Cut **28 slices of lotus root** 1/8-inch thick. Spread meat mixture between two slices of lotus root. Make a batter by mixing **2 eggs,** well beaten, with **1 C. water ;** gradually add this mixture to **1 C. flour** mixed with 1/4 t. salt. Dip sandwiches in batter and fry in deep oil (375°F.) until golden brown, or pan fry. Drain. Serve hot.

PORK AND PEAS

Chu Jou Ch'ao Wan Tou 猪肉炒豌豆

Heat pan and fry until done **1/2 lb. uncooked pork,** sliced fine, adding a small amount of oil if necessary. Add **2 T. soy sauce** and **1 T. sherry.** Set aside.

Sauté **7 dried mushrooms,** cut lengthwise, in **1 T. oil.** Add to meat. Add **2/3 C. soup stock, 1 C. snow peas** or frozen or canned peas, and a mixture of **1 T. cornstarch** and **2 T. water.** Heat thoroughly, stirring slowly, and serve hot. Serves 4.

In ordinary life you must be economical; when you invite guests you must be lavish in hospitality.

居家不可不儉 請客不可不豐

7

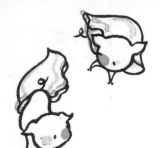

PORK DUMPLINGS

Chiao Tzu 餃子

Doily Batter

Mix **4 C. sifted flour** with enough **warm water** to make a soft dough. Knead until smooth and let stand 1/2 hour before rolling out. Form into long rolls, 1 inch thick ; cut into 1/2 inch pieces ; flatten and roll out very thin and round. If they are made in advance, sprinkle them with cornstarch and stack in refrigerator or in deep freeze. Also the filled Chiao Tzu may be frozen before frying.

Filling

Mix the following ingredients in the order given: **1/2 lb. uncooked pork,** ground, **1/2 head cabbage,** chopped fine and water pressed out, **1/2 C. onion,** chopped fine, **1 T. ginger,** chopped, **2 T. sesame oil** or peanut oil, **3 T. soy sauce,** and **1/2 t. salt.**

Fill each doily with 1 t. of the uncooked filling ; fold over and pinch the edges together. Drop the Chiao Tzu in boiling water. Let come to a rapid boil and add 1/2 C. cold water ; boil again and add another 1/2 C. cold water. Boil again and repeat a third time, adding another 1/2 C. cold water. After the third boiling, serve the Chiao Tzu with soy sauce and a little vinegar, or in any other way desired.

Be sure to boil the Chiao Tzu three times in order to cook the pork thoroughly. After the Chiao Tzu are cooked in this manner they may be fried or served in other ways. Makes about 80 Chiao Tzu.

8

PORK, EGG, AND MUSHROOMS

Ch'ao Mu Hsü Jou 炒木須肉

Dredge **1/2 lb. uncooked lean pork,** sliced fine, with a mixture of **3 T. soy sauce, 1 T. sherry, 1 t. cornstarch,** and **1/2 t. salt.** Heat pan, add **2 T. oil,** and scramble **4 eggs,** beaten. Remove eggs.

Reheat pan ; add **2 T. oil** and sauté for a few seconds the pork and **12 dried mushrooms,** sliced. Add **3 T. water** and scrambled eggs and continue to sauté for a minute. Serves 4 to 6.

Feed moderately on wholesome food ; garden herbs surpass rich viands.

飲食約而精園蔬筵珍饈

PORK WITH CELERY

Chu Jou Szu Ch'ao Chin Ts'ai 豬肉絲炒芹菜

Heat pan, add **2 T. oil**, and fry for a few seconds **2 C. celery**, sliced diagonally. Add **2 T. soy sauce**, **1 t. sherry**, and **1/4 C. soup stock**. Remove from pan.

Dredge **1/2 lb. uncooked lean pork**, sliced thin, with a mixture of **1 t. sherry**, **2 T. cornstarch**, and **1 T. soy sauce**. Reheat pan, add **2 T. oil**, and at once add dredged pork; sauté until done. Add celery and heat thoroughly. Serve at once. Serves 4.

If you rattle your chopsticks against the bowl, you and your descendants will always be poor.

敲碗敲筷窮死萬代

10

PORK WITH CUCUMBERS

Chu Jou Ch'ao Huang Kua 猪肉炒黄瓜

Dredge **1/2 lb. uncooked pork,** cut in small pieces, with a mixture of **1/2 t. cornstarch** and **2 T. soy sauce.** Heat pan, add **1 T. oil** and dredged pork; sauté a few seconds.

Add **1/2 C. water** and simmer until pork is tender (a few minutes). Now add **3 cucumbers,** about 4 inches long, peeled, quartered, and cut in 1-inch pieces. Heat thoroughly. Serve hot. Serves 4.

Better slight a guest than starve him.
寧可慢客不可餓客

11

PORK WITH BAMBOO SHOOTS

Chu Jou Szu Ch'ao Chu Sun 猪肉炒竹筍

In **6 T. oil** sauté for 2 minutes or less **2 C. bamboo shoots** (cooked or canned), sliced lengthwise; remove from pan and drain.

Dredge **1/2 lb. uncooked lean pork,** cut in fine slices, with mixture of **2 T. soy sauce, 1/2 t. salt, 2 T. sherry,** and **1 T. cornstarch.** Reheat pan, add **2 T. oil** and at once add the dredged pork; sauté until tender. Add the sautéed shoots and **1/4 C. water.** Heat thoroughly and serve hot. Serves 4.

Better that a man should wait for his meal than the meal should wait for the man.

寧 人 等 粥 勿 粥 等 人

12

WAN TON

Hun T'ung 餛飩

Use the same type of doily as those for spring rolls, but be careful to pinch the edges together tightly ; or the doilies for *Chiao Tzu* may be used. Fill with Spring Roll filling or with *Wan Ton* filling, as given below.

Mix the following ingredients and fry until the pork is well done : **1/2 lb. uncooked pork**, ground, **2 T. soy sauce**, **1/2 T. sesame oil** or any vegetable oil, **1/4 t. salt**, **4 T. onion**, minced, and **1/2 t. fresh ginger**, chopped.

Use 1/2 t. of the filling for each doily. Fold as illustrated, sealing edges with a mixture of **1 T. cornstarch** and **1/2 C. cold water**. Cook in **6 C. soup stock** until thoroughly done (about 20 minutes.) Serve hot as soup. Serves 6 to 8.

Wan Ton may also be fried in deep oil until golden brown. Serve as hors d'oeuvres or as main dinner dish. They may also be boiled in plain water.

moisten top

filling

fold up, seal top

fold up again

bring these two edges together, moisten, & seal

the result looks like a Dutch cap

SAUTÉED SLICED PORK

Ch'ao P'ien Jo 炒片肉

Fry until done **3/4 lb. uncooked pork,*** cut fine. Add **1 C. onions,** coarsely chopped, and **12 dried mushrooms,** cut in strips. Cook a few seconds. Add **1 C. celery,** cut in 1-inch pieces, and **2 green peppers,** sliced. Cook a few seconds. Add **4 T. soy sauce, 1/2 lb. bean sprouts, 1/2 can water chestnuts** (336 grams), sliced, **1 T. fresh ginger,** chopped fine, and **1/2 C. water.** Thicken with **2 T. cornstarch** mixed with **2 T. water.** Heat thoroughly. Vegetables should be "crunchy." Serves 8.

*This recipe is good made with chicken instead of pork.

14

STUFFED CUCUMBER HALVES

Huang Kua P'ien 黄瓜片

Mix **1 lb. uncooked pork,** veal, or chicken, ground, with **1 T. oil,** 1/2 t. salt, **1 T. soy sauce, 1 T. cornstarch, 3 T. onion,** finely diced, **1/2 C. dried mushrooms,** chopped, and **1 T. fresh ginger,** chopped.

Remove alternate strips of cucumber-peel lengthwise from **6 cucumbers,** each about 7 inches long. This helps the cooked cucumber to hold its shape. Cut in half lengthwise and then crosswise in 2-inch pieces. Scoop out seeds and refill with the meat mixture.*

In a large pan place **2 T. oil.** Arrange the stuffed cucumbers and add **1 C. bouillon.** Cover pan tightly and cook over moderate heat for 10 minutes. Lower the heat and cook another 35 minutes or bake in oven at 325°F. for 35 minutes. Remove cucumbers from pan. In the same pan blend together **2 T. cornstarch, 2 T. soy sauce,** and **1 C. water.** Cook a few minutes stirring constantly until sauce thickens. Pour over the cucumbers and serve at once. Serves 6.

* May be made in advance to this point.

SPRING ROLLS

Ch'un Chüan 春捲

These delightful tidbits may be made with pork, chicken, shrimp, ham, veal, etc. They are fine as hors d'oeuvres or as part of a dinner. The doilies may be made in advance; a supply in the deep freeze is most useful. Sprinkle cornstarch between the doilies before freezing; they can then be peeled off like sheets of paper from a tablet. Or the filled spring rolls may be frozen before frying.

Doily Batter with Eggs

Make a batter, beating **2 eggs** with **2 3/4 C. water,** and adding **2 C. flour.** Beat until smooth. Grease a 7-inch frying pan with a very small amount of oil. Heat pan. Pour a little batter in the pan, swish it around, and pour off excess, leaving a very thin layer of batter in the pan. Leave it on the heat just long enough to set, about one minute or less. Remove from pan and continue to make the next doily.

Eggless Doily Batter

Add **1 1/2 C. water** to **2 C. flour** slowly, making a smooth thin batter. Grease a 7-inch frying pan with a very small mount of oil. Heat pan, and brush on the batter with a pastry brush, preferably in a 5-inch square. If holes appear, brush on more batter with crosswise strokes. Leave it on the heat just long enough to set, about one minute or less. Remove from pan and continue to make the next doily.

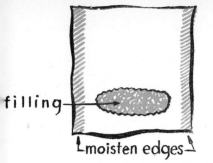

filling—

└moisten edges┘

┌urn up bottom
over filling

Spring Roll Filling

In **1 T. oil** sauté slightly **2 C. bamboo shoots,** cut in strips lengthwise. Add **3 C. uncooked bean sprouts** or 1 can bean sprouts (1 lb.), drained, and heat thoroughly. Add **2 T. soy sauce** and continue to sauté the bamboo shoots and bean sprouts a few seconds; remove from pan.

Reheat pan, add **1 T. oil,** and sauté **2 T. onion,** and **1/2 C. dried mushrooms,** cut in strips; remove from pan. Dredge **1 lb. uncooked lean pork,** ground, with a mixture of **1 T. soy sauce, 1 T. sherry, 1 T. cornstarch,** and **1 t. salt.** Reheat pan, add **1 T. oil** and sauté the dredged pork thoroughly. Add the vegetables and **1 T. fresh ginger,** chopped. Cool.

Spread 1 1/2 t. of the meat and vegetable mixture on each doily. Fold sides in and roll (see illustration). Moisten edges of doily with a mixture of **1 T. cornstarch** and **1/2 C. cold water.** Heat oil for deep-fat frying (390°F.) and fry rolls until brown. Drain. One recipe of filling makes about 45 to 50 rolls.

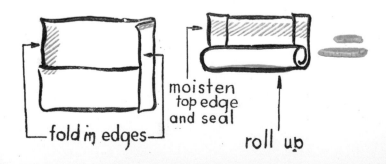

└fold in edges┘

moisten
top edge
and seal

roll up

TAIWANESE SPECIAL

Tai Wan T'e Pieh 台湾特別

Heat pan, add **3 T. oil** and **1 lb. uncooked pork,** cut in small pieces; fry until well done. Add **2 C. onions,** coarsely chopped, and sauté slightly; add **3 T. soy sauce** and **1/2 large head cabbage,** finely shredded, and give it a few turns. Add **1 t. sugar, 1 T. fresh ginger,** chopped, and **3 green peppers,** sliced. Add **salt,** if necessary. Heat thoroughly and serve at once with rice, boiled noodles, or crisp noodles.

The cabbage, onions, and peppers should be "crunchy." Do not overcook. If liquid forms, thicken it with **1 T. cornstarch** mixed with **1/4 C. water.** Serves 4 to 6.

Note: Instead of pork, fish fillets may be used.

PORK WITH VEGETABLES

Chu Jou Ch'ao Ts'ai 猪肉炒菜

Fry until done **1/2 lb. uncooked shoulder pork,** thinly shredded. Add **1 C. onions,** sliced lengthwise, and sauté a few seconds. In another pan sauté **2 C. bamboo shoots,** shredded, in **1/2 T. oil;** add to meat. In **1/2 T. oil** sauté **7 dried mushrooms,** sliced; add to meat.*

Mix **4 T. soy sauce, 1 T. sugar, 1 T. cornstarch,** and **1/2 C. mushroom water** or soup stock. Add to meat. Cook a few minutes, stirring slowly, and add **1 T. fresh ginger,** chopped fine, and **8 water chestnuts,** sliced lengthwise, Heat thoroughly and serve hot. Serves 4.

* May be made in advance to this point.

SWEET-SOUR PORK OR SPARERIBS

Suan T'ien Chu Jou 酸甜豚肉

Make sweet-sour sauce in advance. Mix **3/4 C. sugar,** **1/4 C. soy sauce, 1/3 C. vinegar, 2/3 C. water,** and **3 T. cornstarch.** Cook over low heat until thickened, stirring constantly.

Place in a kettle **2 lbs. uncooked pork** or spareribs, cut in pieces about 1 inch thick and 2 inches long. Add **1 C. cold water** and boil 20 minutes or until tender. Pour off water, if there is any left. Cool.

While meat is cooling, sauté **1/4 C. onion,** sliced, and **1 medium cucumber,** peeled and sliced, for one minute in **2 T. oil.** (If cucumbers are not available, equivalent amounts of any one of the following may be used: green pepper, pineapple, bamboo shoots, carrots, crab apples.) Remove from pan. Now add to the cool pork a mixture of **2 T. soy sauce** and **2 T. cornstarch.** Heat oil for deep-fat frying (390°F.) and fry the meat until crisp and brown. Remove and drain. Combine meat with hot sweet-sour sauce and sautéed vegetables. (More sugar may be added to suit the taste.) Serves 4 to 6.

Fowl

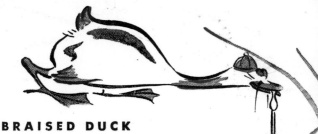

BRAISED DUCK

Hung Shao Ya 紅燒鴨

Clean well **1 duck** (about 3 lbs.) or equivalent amount of wild duck or duck cut in pieces; remove oil sacs. Mix **1 T. fresh ginger**, chopped fine, **2 T. sherry**, and **1 C. onions**, chopped, and rub the duck inside and out with this mixture. Let it stand about one half hour.

Heat **1/2 C. oil** and fry the duck until light brown; drain. Place the browned duck in a heavy kettle or pan and pour over it **1/2 C. soy sauce, 1 t. sugar,** and **2 C. water.** Bring to a boil, then simmer about 1 1/2 hours or until until duck is tender. It may be necessary to add more water if the duck is a tough one! Serves 4.

CHESTNUT CHICKEN

Li Tzu Chi 栗子雞

Cut **1 lb. uncooked chicken meat** into 1-inch pieces. Heat pan, add **1 T. oil,** sauté **2 C. onions,** sliced lengthwise, until light brown, and remove. Reheat pan, add **1 T. oil,** and sauté chicken until slightly brown; add **6 dried mushrooms,** sliced, and continue to sauté.

Mix **4 T. soy sauce, 1 t. salt, 1 T. sugar, 1 T. sherry,** and **1 T. cornstarch;** add to chicken and stir until thickened. Add onions, **2 1/2 C. hot water, 1 T. fresh ginger,** chopped, and **30 chestnuts,** boiled 20 to 30 minutes and peeled. Simmer until chicken is tender. Serve hot. Serves 6 to 8.

CHICKEN WITH EGGPLANT

Chi Ch'ieh Tze 雞茄子

Cover **4 C. eggplant,** cut in shoestring strips, with **boiling water;** let stand 5 minutes; drain well.

Dredge **1/2 lb. uncooked chicken meat,** cut in shoestring strips, with a mixture of **1 T. cornstarch, 2 T. soy sauce,** and **1 T. sherry.** Heat pan; add **4 T. oil;** sauté **5 hot peppers,** shredded fine with seeds removed, until they turn color. Remove from pan. In the same pan sauté the chicken until done. Add eggplant, **1 small clove garlic,** chopped fine, sautéed peppers, **1 T. fresh ginger,** chopped, and **1/2 C. soup stock.** Heat thoroughly. Serves 6.

This entire recipe may be made in advance and reheated before serving.

25

CHICKEN WITH VEGETABLES

Chi Ch'ao Ts'ai 雞炒菜

Dredge **1 lb. uncooked chicken meat,** cut in cubes, with a mixture of **1 T. cornstarch, 2 T. sherry, 1 t. salt, 1/4 C. water, 1/2 C. onion,** chopped, and **2 T. fresh ginger,** chopped.

In **4 T. oil** sauté for 2 minutes **1 C. dried mushrooms,** cut in cubes, and **1 C. bamboo shoots,** cut in cubes; remove from pan. Reheat pan; add **4 T. oil** and the dredged chicken; sauté until tender.* Now add the sautéed mushrooms and bamboo shoots, **4 T. soy sauce, 1 C. snow peas** or fresh or frozen peas, and **1 C. water chestnuts,** cubed. Heat thoroughly and serve hot. Serves 4 to 6.

* May be made in advance to this point.

CHICKEN VELVET

Chi Jung 鶏芙

To **1/2 C. uncooked chicken breast**, ground, add **1 t. cornstarch**, **1/4 t. salt**, and **1 unbeaten egg white.** Mix well and slowly add **1/4 C. water**, a few drops at a time. (If water is added too fast, the mixture will not hold together.) Beat **4 egg whites** until stiff and gradually fold into the chicken mixture.

Heat pan, add **2 T. oil** or chicken fat, and let it heat only to melting if solid fat has been used. Pour the chicken and egg white mixture into the pan, remove from fire at once, and stir the mixture rapidly. After the fat is stirred into the mixture, replace on fire, and cook until firm but not browned. The mixture should just "set."

The gravy may be prepared beforehand. Pour the hot gravy over the Chicken Velvet. Heat thoroughly and serve hot. Serves 4.

Gravy

Mix **1 C. rich chicken stock**, **1 t. sherry**, **1/4 t. salt**, and **1 T. cornstarch;** heat thoroughly.

Notes: May be prepared in advance and reheated. If chicken fat is used in place of oil, Chicken Velvet is an excellent dish for an invalid.

CHICKEN AND TOMATOES

Chi Ting Ch'ao Hsi Hung Shih 鷄丁炒西紅柿

Cut **1 lb. uncooked chicken meat** in 1-inch squares. Dredge it with a mixture of **1 T. soy sauce, 1 T. sherry,** and **1 T. cornstarch.**

Heat pan, add **1/2 C. oil;** sauté dredged chicken until tender. Add **1 C. onions,** cubed, and fry a few seconds. Drain chicken and onion. Reheat pan, add **2 T. of the drained oil, 1 T. soy sauce, 1 T. cornstarch, 1/4 t. salt, 1 t. sugar,** and **1/2 C. soup stock** or water. Boil a few seconds.* To the boiling sauce add chicken, onions, and finally **2 medium sized tomatoes,** peeled and cubed. Heat thoroughly and serve hot. Serves 6.

* May be made in advance to this point.

LOQUAT CHICKEN

Li Chih Chi 荔枝鶏

Mix together **1 lb. uncooked chicken meat,** ground, **3 T. onion,** chopped fine, and **10 water chestnuts,** chopped fine, or 6 dried mushrooms, chopped. Add **2 T. cornstarch,** 1/2 t. salt, **2 T. soy sauce, 1 T. sherry,** and **2 egg whites,** stiffly beaten. Form into 18 balls the size of a large walnut. Fry the balls in deep oil until brown. Drain.

Heat pan, add **1 T. oil, 1 C. loquat juice,** 1/2 C. **chicken stock,** and **2 T. soy sauce** mixed with **2 T. cornstarch ;** cook a few seconds.* Add chicken balls and **1 can loquats** (850 grams), drained. Heat thoroughly and serve hot. Serves 6 to 8.

* May be made in advance to this point.

MUSHROOM CHICKEN

K'ou Mo Chi Ting 口蘑鷄丁

Dredge **1 lb. uncooked chicken meat,** cut in 1-inch squares, with a mixture of **1/2 C. soy sauce, 2 T. sugar,** and **5 T. cornstarch.** Put **2 cans mushrooms** (3 oz. each) in a saucepan over low heat. When it boils, add the dredged chicken. Gradually add **2 C. soup stock** and cook until chicken is tender. Serve hot. Serves 6.

Note: If mushroom juice is too salty, pour it off and use an equal amount of water in place of it. If fresh mushrooms are used, sauté them first.

He who cannot in his own house entertain a guest, when abroad will find few to entertain him.

在家不會迎賓客出外方知少主人

PINEAPPLE CHICKEN

Po Lo Chi 菠蘿鷄

Dredge **1 lb. uncooked chicken meat,** cut in 1-inch pieces, with a mixture of **1 T. cornstarch, 1 t. salt, 2 t. cold water,** and **1 T. soy sauce.** Sauté **1 1/2 C. onions,** sliced lengthwise, in **1 T. oil** for 2 minutes and remove from pan. Sauté **1 C. celery,** cut diagonally, and **10 water chestnuts,** sliced lengthwise, in **1 T. oil** for 2 minutes or less and remove from pan. Sauté the dredged chicken in **2 T. oil** until brown.*

Add the vegetables, **4 large slices of canned pineapple,** cut in wedges, and finally **4 T. pineapple juice** to the chicken and simmer until thoroughly heated. Serve hot with rice. Serves 6.

* Beef or pork may be substituted for the chicken. The vegetables should be crisp and not cooked soft.

PEPPERED CHICKEN

La Tzu Chi 辣子鸡

Dredge **1 lb. uncooked chicken meat,** cut in 1 1/2-inch pieces, with a mixture of **1 T. cornstarch** and **1 T. soy sauce.** Fry chicken in deep oil until brown and tender. Drain.

Cube **2 C. onions, 1 cucumber** about 7 inches long, **4 green peppers, 2 sweet red peppers,** and **1 hot pepper,** with seeds removed; dredge in a mixture of **2 T. cornstarch, 3 T. soy sauce, 1 t. sugar, 1/2 t. salt,** and **1/4 C. soup stock** or water. Fry the dredged vegetables slightly in **2 T. oil,** stirring constantly.* Combine meat and vegetables. Serve hot. Serves 4 to 6.

* May be made in advance to this point.

WALNUT CHICKEN

Ho T'ao Chi Ting 核桃鶏丁

Cube **1 C. bamboo shoots, 1 C. celery, 1 C. onions,** and **8 water chestnuts ;** sauté them slightly in **3 T. oil.** Remove from pan. Brown **1/2 lb. (2 C.) walnut meats** or almonds, blanched, in deep oil ; remove and drain.

Dredge **1 lb. uncooked chicken meat,** cut in cubes, with a mixture of **3/4 t. salt, 2 T. cornstarch, 3 T. soy sauce, 2 T. sherry,** and **1 t. sugar.** Heat pan ; add **3 T. oil** and sauté the dredged chicken until it is tender. To the chicken add **1/4 C. soup stock** and heat thoroughly.* Add vegetables and walnuts, heat thoroughly, and serve hot. Serves 4 to 6.

Special Note on Walnuts : To remove the bitter flavor of shelled walnuts, cover them with cold water, bring to a boil, and boil 3 minutes. Drain immediately.

* May be made in advance to this point.

Beef

BEEF AND ONIONS

Niu Jou Ch'ao Ts'ung 牛肉炒葱

Heat **2 T. oil** and sauté slightly **3 C. onion rings,** thinly sliced. Add **1 T. soy sauce, 1/2 t. sugar,** and **1 t. sherry;** continue to heat a second or two. Remove from pan.

Dredge **1/2 lb. tender beef** (top round), sliced fine, with mixture of **2 t. cornstarch, 1 T. soy sauce,** and **1 t. sherry.** Heat pan, add **2 T. oil,** and sauté beef.*

Add onions to the beef. Heat thoroughly and serve hot. Serves 4.

* May be made in advance to this point.

BEEF WITH CAULIFLOWER AND SNOW PEAS

Niu Jou Ch'ao Ts'ai Hua Wan Tou
牛肉炒菜花豌豆

In **2 T. oil** brown **1 clove garlic** and remove. Add **1 lb. beef,** cut in small thin slices, and sauté until brown. Add **4 T. onions,** chopped, **2 t. salt,** and a **dash of pepper ;** cook a few seconds.

Add **1 C. bouillon, 1 medium cauliflower,** broken in pieces, and **1 lb. snow peas** or fresh or frozen peas. Cook about 5 minutes or until cauliflower and peas are thoroughly heated but not soft.

Add mixture of **2 T. cornstarch, 2 T. soy sauce,** and **1/2 C. water ;** cook a few minutes longer to thicken, stirring slowly. Serve hot. Serves 6 to 8.

BEEF WITH PEPPERS

Niu Jou Ch'ao La Tzu 牛肉炒辣子

Heat pan; add **1 1/2 T. oil** and **1 clove garlic**, crushed, (optional). When garlic turns brown, remove. Add **1 lb. beef,** cut in small thin pieces, and fry a few minutes. Season with **1 t. salt** and **pepper** to taste. Add **1 C. soup stock** and continue to cook a few seconds.*

Add mixture of **2 T. cornstarch, 1 T. soy sauce,** and **2 T. water.** Cook until sauce thickens, stirring slowly. Add **1 C. green peppers,** sliced lengthwise, and **1/2 t. fresh ginger,** chopped fine. Heat thoroughly and serve hot. Serves 4 to 6.

* May be made in advance to this point.

BEEF WITH RADISHES

Niu Jou Ch'ao Hung Lo Po 牛肉炒紅蘿蔔

Dredge **1/2 lb. beef** sliced very thin and cut in small pieces with mixture of **2 T. soy sauce** and **2 t. cornstarch.** Prepare sweet-sour sauce by combining **2 T. oil, 3 T. vinegar, 6 T. water, 1/2 C. sugar,** and **1 T. cornstarch ;** cook for a few seconds. Add the dredged meat and cook until the meat is done (a few minutes).

Lastly add **8 sliced radishes.** Do not cook the radishes but heat them thoroughly. Serve hot. Serves 4.

Earth has no feasts which do not break up.
天 下 無 不 散 的 筵 席

SWEET-SOUR BEEF BALLS WITH PINEAPPLE AND PEPPERS

Suan T'ien Niu Jou Po Lo La Tzu
酸甜牛肉菠羅辣子

Mix **1 lb. ground beef, 1 egg, 1 T. cornstarch, 1 t. salt, 2 T. onion,** chopped, and a few grains of **pepper ;** form into 18 balls or more. Brown them in a small amount of oil ; drain.

To **1 T. oil** add **1 C. pineapple juice** and cook over low heat a few minutes. Add mixture of **3 T. cornstarch, 1 T. soy sauce, 3 T. vinegar, 6 T. water,** and 1/2 **C. sugar.** Cook until juice thickens, stirring constantly.*

Add meat balls, **4 slices pineapple,** cut in pieces, and **3 large green peppers,** each cut into 12 to 15 strips lengthwise. Heat thoroughly. Serve hot. Serves 6 to 8.

* May be made in advance to this point.

41

STRING BEANS AND BEEF

Niu Jou Szu Ch'ao Pien Tou Szu 牛肉絲炒扁豆絲

Dredge **1/2 lb. tender beef** (top round), thinly sliced, with mixture of **2 T. soy sauce, 1 t. sugar, 1 T. cornstarch, 1/2 t. salt,** and **1 T. sherry.** Heat pan; add **2 T. oil** and sauté the dredged beef a few seconds.

Pour **1 1/2 C. boiling water** over **1/2 lb. string beans,** cut lengthwise; bring to a boil and drain immediately (save 1/4 C. of the water). Add parboiled beans or 1 can string beans (15 1/2 oz.) or 1 package frozen string beans to meat. Add **1/4 C. bean water.** (If frozen beans are used, no additional water is required.) Simmer a few seconds. Serve hot. Serves 4.

Note: Do not overcook the beans; overcooked beans turn yellow and lose flavor.

BEEF WITH MUSHROOMS, ONIONS, AND GINGER

Niu Jou Ch'ao Mo Ku Ts'ung T'ou Sheng Chiang
牛肉炒蘑菇葱頭生薑

Heat **2 T. oil** and sauté **3 C. onions**, cut lengthwise, until slightly brown (not done). Take from pan. Reheat pan; add **2 T. oil** and **1 lb. beef**, ground or cut in fine strips; fry until brown.

Add sautéed onions, **1 can (3 oz.) mushrooms**, drained, **2 T. shredded ginger,** and **4 T. soy sauce**; heat thoroughly. Add **2 T. cornstarch** mixed with **1 C. mushroom juice** (juice from can plus water). Continue to cook a few seconds to thicken, stirring slowly. Serve hot with rice or noodles. Serves 4 to 6.

Intoxication is not the wine's fault, but the man's.
酒 不 醉 人 人 自 醉

Seafood

SWEET-SOUR FISH

Suan T'ien Yü 酸甜魚

Clean any **white fish, 2 1/2 to 3 lbs.,** and make three parallel slashes across the fish on each side at right angles to backbone, slanting toward the tail and leaving the flesh adhering to the bones. Do not cut gashes too close to the tail. Dredge well with a paste made of **3 T. cornstarch** and **3 T. water.**

Heat oil very hot for deep-fat frying. Hold fish over the pan and baste the slashes with the hot oil until brown, before carefully dropping the fish into the pan to fry until crisp (about 15 minutes). Remove fish from pan and drain. Fried pieces of fish will do very well, instead of a whole fish. Serves 4 to 6.

Sweet-Sour Sauce

Mix well **3 T. Oil, 1 C. sugar, 4 T. cornstarch, 4 T. soy sauce, 2/3 C. vinegar,** and **1 1/3 C. water.** Heat. Add **2 C. onion,** chopped, and **1 T. fresh ginger,** chopped; boil one minute. Pour over fish. Serve hot. This sauce may be made in advance and reheated. It may also be used with other meats.

DOLLAR SHRIMP OR SHRIMP BALLS

Hsia Ch'iu 蝦球

Shell, clean, and chop fine **1 lb. uncooked shrimp.**
Add **10 water chestnuts,** chopped fine, and mix
thoroughly. Add **1 T. cornstarch, 1 t. sherry, 1/2 t.
salt,** and **1 egg,** beaten slightly ; mix. Form into balls.
Fry in deep oil until golden brown. Serve hot. Makes
12 to 15 balls.

*Friends while good dinners last; husband and wife while fuel and
food remain.*

酒肉朋友柴米夫妻

48

SHRIMP FOO YUNG

Hsia Jen Ch'ao Foo Yung 蝦仁炒鶏子

Stir (do not beat) together until thick : **1 C. cooked shrimp,** shredded, or 1 can (6 oz.) shrimp, shredded, or any cooked meat, **1 C. onions,** shredded, **1/4 C. water chestnuts,** sliced thin, or bean sprouts, **1/2 C. dried mushrooms,** chopped, **5 eggs,** and **2 t. soy sauce.** Heat a shallow pan with a small amount of **oil.** Drop by spoonsful into the oil. When brown on one side, turn and brown the other. Serve hot. Serves 4.

Sauce

Mix and cook over low heat **1 T. cornstarch, 1 T. soy sauce, 3/4 C. bouilion,** broth, or water, and **1/4 t. sugar.**

SHRIMP AND VEGETABLES

Hsia Jen Ch'ao Ts'ai 蝦仁炒菜

Shell and clean **1 lb. uncooked shrimp ;** dredge with a mixture of **2 T. soy sauce, 1/4 t. salt, 1 t. fresh ginger,** chopped, and **1 T. sherry.** Heat pan, add **2 T. oil,** and sauté the dredged shrimp. Remove from pan.

Reheat pan, add **2 T. oil,** and partly sauté **1 1/2 C. onions,** sliced lengthwise, and **1 C. celery,** cut in 2-inch lengths. Add **12 water chestnuts,** sliced lengthwise, **1/2 lb. (3 C.) fresh bean sprouts** or snow peas or 1 can (1 lb.) drained bean sprouts, and the sautéed shrimp. Add a mixture of **1 T. cornstarch** and **1/2 C. soup stock** or water. Cook until thickened, stirring constantly. Serve hot. Serves 8.

SHRIMP WITH CUCUMBERS

Hsia Jen Ch'ao Huang Kua Pien 蝦仁炒黃瓜片

Peel **3 cucumbers,** quarter them lengthwise, and cut in 2-inch pieces. Shell and clean **1 lb. uncooked shrimp** and dredge with a mixture of **1 T. cornstarch, 1/2 t. salt,** and **1 T. sherry.**

Heat pan, add **2 T. oil,** fry shrimp 3 minutes, and drain. Reheat pan, add **1 T. oil** and cucumbers, and fry a few seconds. Add **2 T. soy sauce, 1 t. sugar,** and **1/2 t. cornstarch** mixed with **1/4 C. water ;** simmer a minute. Add shrimp and heat thoroughly. Serve hot. Serves 4.

SHRIMP ON TOAST

K'ao Hsia Mi Mien Pao 烤蝦米麵包

Chop very fine **1 lb. uncooked shrimp** and **4 T. onion**; season with **1/2 t. salt** and a **dash of pepper**. Add **1 unbeaten egg white** and **1 t. cornstarch**. Mix well. Spread on thin **squares of bread** and fry in deep oil until golden brown. Serve hot. Cut them very small for hors d'oeuvres. Serves 4 to 6.

Whilst travelling don't reckon the distance; whilst eating don't reckon the quantity.

行不計路食不計數

BRAISED PRAWNS OR SHRIMP

Shao Tui Hsia 燒對蝦

Shell and clean **1 1/2 lb. uncooked prawns** or shrimp; cut into 1-inch pieces. Fry them in **4 T. oil** until color changes to light red; add **4 T. soy sauce, 1 T. sugar,** and **1 1/2 T. sherry.** Continue to fry a few seconds. Add **2 t. fresh ginger,** chopped fine, **1 C. onions,** sliced lengthwise, and **1 C. bamboo shoots** or cucumbers, sliced lengthwise, and cook slightly. Add a mixture of **1/4 C. water** and **1 t. cornstarch.** Continue to cook for 2 minutes, stirring slowly. Serves 4.

An eating-house keeper doesn't care how big your appetite is.
開 飯 店 的 不 怕 係 肚 子 大

Vegetables

ASPARAGUS PEKING STYLE

Lung Hsu Ts'ai 龍鬚菜

Heat pan, add **2 T. oil, 1/4 C. chicken stock, 1/4 C. water, 1 T. sherry, 2 T. soy sauce,** and **1 T. corn-starch.** Stir constantly until it boils. Now add **1 can asparagus** (14 1/2 oz.), drained; heat thoroughly. Serve hot. This is very good with Western-style meat. Serves 4 or 5.

Let there be plenty of food and clothing, and propriety and righteousness will flourish.

衣食足而後禮義興

BAMBOO SHOOTS AND MUSHROOMS

Chu Sun Ch'ao Mo Ku 竹筍炒蘑菇

In **8 T. oil** sauté for a few seconds **2 C. bamboo shoots,** cut into lengthwise slices. Drain. In **2 T. oil** sauté **12 dried mushrooms,** cut in strips. Add **4 T. soy sauce, 1 T. sherry,** and **1 T. sugar.**

Now add the sautéed bamboo shoots and **1/4 C. mushroom water** mixed with **1 t. cornstarch.** Simmer a few minutes, stirring slowly. Serve hot. Serves 4 or 5.

Good wine reddens the face; riches excite the mind.
好酒紅人面財帛動人心

BAMBOO SHOOTS AND SOY SAUCE

Chu Sun T'ien Chiang Yu 竹筍糖醬油

Cut **2 C. bamboo shoots** into slices, lengthwise and once across. Heat **oil** and deep-fat fry bamboo shoots only to a very slight degree. Drain the shoots. Reheat them, add **5 T. soy sauce,** and mix well into the shoots. Now add a mixture of **3 T. sugar, 1 T. corn-starch,** and **1/2 C. water.** Simmer gently for a few minutes. Additional water may be added if necessary. Serve hot. Good with Western-style meats. Serves 6 to 8.

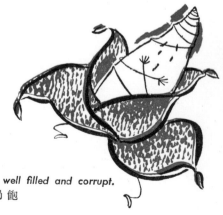

Better be hungry and pure than well filled and corrupt.
寧可清饑不可濁飽

CAULIFLOWER, WATER CHESTNUTS, AND MUSHROOMS

Ts'ai Hua Pi Ch'i Mo Ku 菜花荸薺磨菇

Parboil **1 medium cauliflower,** broken into pieces, by pouring boiling water over it and letting it stand for 5 minutes. Drain well.

Heat pan, add **2 T. oil,** and sauté **5 dried mushrooms,** sliced, a few seconds. Add **6 water chestnuts,** each sliced into four pieces, **1/2 C. mushroom water,** **1/4 C. soup stock,** **1 t. sherry,** **2 T. soy sauce, 2 T. cornstarch,** and **1 t. oil.** Simmer a few seconds, stirring constantly. Add the cauliflower and heat thoroughly. Cauliflower should be " crunchy." Serve hot. Serves 4.

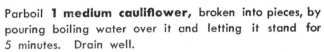

SPINACH AND MUSHROOMS

Po Ts'ai Men Mo Ku 波菜燗蕃菇

Heat pan, add **3 T. oil,** and sauté **14 dried mushrooms,** sliced, until slightly brown. Add **4 T. soy sauce, 1 T. sherry, 1 T. sugar, 1/2 t. salt,** and heat for a few seconds. Add **1 C. mushroom water** and simmer until mushrooms are tender. Add a mixture of **1 T. cornstarch** and **1 T. water** and cook until it thickens, stirring slowly.

Wash **1 lb. fresh spinach** and shake off excess water; or use 1 package (10 oz.) frozen spinach. Put in a kettle over low heat. Turn spinach with your fingers until too hot to handle. Leave a second longer. Take from fire and place spinach on a platter. Pour cooked mushrooms and gravy over the spinach. Serve hot. Serves 4.

Soup

MANDARIN SOUP

Peiping T'ang 北平湯

Sauté slightly **1 C. raw lean pork,** cut in strips. Add **1 C. mushrooms, 1/2 C. carrots,** diced, and **1 C. celery,** chopped. Continue to sauté until vegetables are tender. Add **6 C. bouillon,** beef or chicken, heated. Add **1/2 C. chopped spinach** and **1 t. Aji-no-Moto.** Bring to a boil, add **1 egg,** slightly beaten, and stir quickly. Then add **2 T. cornstarch** made into a thin paste with a little **water.** Season with **salt** and **pepper** to taste. Serve hot. Serves 6.

Clothes and food are daily mercies.
衣飯逐日生

CRAB SOUP

P'ang T'ang 蟹湯

Warm slightly **4 T. oil** ; add **3 slices fresh ginger,** each 1 inch in diameter, and **1/2 C. onion,** chopped fine. Sauté about 1 minute. Add **1/2 C. crab meat,** canned or fresh, **1/4 t. salt,** and **1 T. sherry.** Continue to cook 1 minute. Add **4 C. chicken stock** and bring to a boil. Remove the ginger.

Combine **2 egg whites,** beaten, with **1/4 C. light cream,** add **2 t. cornstarch** mixed with **2 T. cold water,** and gradually add to the crab meat mixture, stirring constantly. Simmer gently about 1 minute and serve at once. Serves 4.

EGG SOUP

Chi Tzu T'ang 鶏蛋湯

Heat **2 C. chicken stock** or consommé to boiling, dribble **1 egg,** well stirred, gradually into the stock, stirring constantly. Add **1 t. soy sauce** and **1/4 t. salt.** (Do not add salt if consommé is used.) One thinly sliced **green onion** may be floated on the soup. Serves 2 or 3.

Diligence and economy secure plenty to eat and drink; whilst idleness and sloth bring hunger and starvation.

勤 儉 勤 儉 茶 飯 隨 便 慵 惰 慵 惰 忍 饑 受 餓

Desserts

NOTE

While Westerners like Chinese food, we have found that they do not care much for most Chinese desserts. So we have concocted some Western-style desserts that go particularly well with Chinese food. You will find them in this section along with purely Chinese desserts.

CARAMEL SQUARES

Hung T'ang Kao 紅糖粞

Cream together **1/2 C. shortening** and **1/2 C. sugar.** Add **3 egg yolks** and **1 egg white;** beat well. Add **1 t. vanilla, 1 C. flour** sifted with **1 t. baking powder, 1/4 t. salt,** and **3 T. milk.** Spread this mixture in a well-greased pan, about 12″ × 8″ × 2″. Sprinkle with **3/4 C. nuts,** finely cut.

Beat **2 egg whites** until stiff. Add **1 3/4 C. light brown sugar** and **1/2 t. vanilla.** Spread this mixture over the nuts. Bake about 30 minutes at 350°F. Cut in squares while warm. Makes 15 squares.

COCONUT DREAMS

Yeh Tzu Kao 椰子糕

Mix thoroughly **1/2 C. shortening, 1/2 C. brown sugar,** and **1 1/3 C. sifted flour;** press into well-greased baking pan 8″ × 12″. Bake at 325°F. for 20 minutes.

For top mixture make a batter of **2 eggs, 1/8 t. salt, 1 C. brown sugar, 1 t. vanilla, 3 T. flour,** and **1/2 t. baking powder.** Beat well; add **1 C. chopped nuts.** Spread over the partly baked bottom mixture and sprinkle with **1 C. shredded coconut.** Bake about 25 minutes at 325°F. until browned. Cut into bars, squares, or sticks while warm. Cool in pan. Serve warm or cold. May be frozen. Makes 12 to 15 squares.

DREAM BARS

Meng Hsiang Ping 夢想餅

Mix **1 C. sifted flour** and **2 T. brown sugar.** Cut in **1/2 C. butter** or margarine until mixture becomes crumbly. Put into greased pan 8″×12″. Bake at 350°F. for 15 minutes.

For top mixture sift together **1/4 C. flour, 1/2 t. baking powder,** and **1/8 t. salt.** Beat **2 eggs** well and add **1 1/2 C. brown sugar;** add to dry ingredients. Add **1 t. vanilla, 3/4 C. shredded coconut,** and **1 package semi-sweet chocolate nibs** (6 oz.). Spread on baked mixture. Bake 20 minutes at 350°F. Cut into bars. Makes 15 to 18 bars.

CREAM PUFF PIE

Nai Yu Ch'i Wa Kuo Ping 奶油气凸鍋餅

Mix **1/2 C. boiling water, 1/4 C. shortening,** and **1/8 t. salt** over heat. Stir in **1/2 C. flour** all at once. Stir constantly until mixture leaves the sides of the pan and forms into a ball (about one minute). Remove from fire; cool slightly. Beat in **2 eggs,** one at a time, beating until smooth after each addition. Beat mixture until smooth and velvety. Spread in greased 9-inch pie pan (don't spread on sides) or casserole. Bake 50 to 60 minutes at 400°F. Sides will rise up and curl in slightly. When baked, allow to cool slowly away from drafts.

Fill with the following: Mix **3/4 C. sugar, 1/3 C. flour,** and **1/8 t. salt.** Beat in **2 eggs** and gradually add **2 C. scalded milk.** Cook in double boiler about 10 minutes, or carefully over a low fire, being careful not to burn; stir constantly until mixture thickens. Take from fire; cool, add **1 t. vanilla.** Fold in **1 C. whipped cream.** Pour cream filling into crust and top with **1 C. whipped cream.** Decorate with well-sweetened **strawberries** or other fruit in season. May be frozen after filling is added to crust. Serves 8 to 10.

DUETTE DEW

T'ien Kuo Fu Ju T'i 天国夫如替

Beat **2 eggs** and add **3/4 C. sugar**, **1/4 C. evaporated milk** or cream, **1/2 lb. dates,** cut in pieces, and **1 C. nuts,** chopped. Mix **3 T. flour**, **1 t. baking powder,** and **1/8 t. salt** and add to the above mixture. Pour into a well-greased pan 8″ × 12″. Bake 20 minutes at 325°F. When cool, pick apart into small pieces with fork and pile on plate or in individual dishes. Add whipped cream, then more pieces of the the cake. Do not mix. Top with whipped cream and a maraschino cherry. The recipe should use about **2 C. whipped cream.** Serves 6 to 8.

Cake may be made several days in advance. Add cream before serving.

EIGHT PRECIOUS PUDDING

Pa Pao Fan 八寶飯

Wash **1 1/2 C. uncooked rice** and cook in **6 C. cold water** until soft. Do not drain. Add **1/2 C. sugar** and mix.

Grease well an 8-inch bowl or deep pan. Arrange three-fourths of the following fruits and nuts in any pattern in the bowl; **12 dates,** pitted, **1 C. candied fruit** or glazed fruit cake mix, **1 C. blanched walnuts** or almonds, **1 C. raisins.** Place cooked rice in this bowl, being careful not to spoil the fruit pattern. Add the remaining one-fourth of the fruit and nuts across the top of the rice. Cover tightly with foil or waxed paper and steam 30 minutes. Remove bowl by inverting it over a platter and serve hot with sauce. Pudding may be frozen before or after steaming. Serves 10 to 12.

Sauce

Mix and boil for a few minutes **1 C. sugar, 2 T. cornstarch,** and **1 C. water.** Pour over pudding.

76

HONEYED FRUIT

Pa Szu Hsiang Chiao, P'ing Kuo 拔絲香蕉，萍果

Peel and core **2 large apples.** Slice each apple in 12 lengthwise pieces. Bananas may also be used. Make a batter of **1/2 C. egg whites,** unbeaten, **3 T. cornstarch,** and **3 T. flour.** Add fruit to batter and mix until each piece is coated. Deep-fat fry the coated fruit slices until light brown. Do not have the oil too hot. Drain.*

Make a syrup of **4 T. oil, 1 C. water, 2 C. sugar,** and **1 T. Karo syrup.** Boil it to 240° F. (firm soft ball). Add the fruit and cook until the syrup turns brown and starts to caramelize (about 3 or 4 minutes). Stir the fruit gently all the time and be careful not to let the syrup burn. During the last minute of cooking, add **1 T. black sesame seeds** or a few chopped nuts. Pour syrup and fruit onto a well-greased platter. To serve, pick up a fruit slice with chopsticks, dip it quickly into **cold water,** and eat. Serves 4 to 6.

* May be made in advance to this point.

LEMON SPONGE PUDDING

Hsiang T'ao Ping 香桃餅

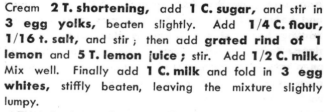

Cream **2 T. shortening,** add **1 C. sugar,** and stir in **3 egg yolks,** beaten slightly. Add **1/4 C. flour, 1/16 t. salt,** and stir ; then add **grated rind of 1 lemon** and **5 T. lemon juice ;** stir. Add **1/2 C. milk.** Mix well. Finally add **1 C. milk** and fold in **3 egg whites,** stiffly beaten, leaving the mixture slightly lumpy.

Turn the batter into a well-greased baking dish holding 1 1/2 to 2 quarts, set the dish in a shallow pan of hot water, and bake at 350°F. for 45 minutes or until golden brown. May also be baked in individual dishes. Serve hot or cold, with or without whipped cream. Serves 8 to 10.

For Lemon Sponge Pie, add mixture to raw pie crust and bake.

78

MERINGUE NESTS

Tan Ch'ing P'i Wo 蛋青皮窩

Add a **few grains of salt** to **1/2 C. egg whites** and beat until stiff; add **3/4 C. sugar** by tablespoons, beating well between each addition; lastly add **4 drops lemon extract.** Place meringue by spoonsful on a cookie sheet lined with two layers of heavy brown paper, shape in the form of nests, and bake at 300°F. until a delicate golden color (12 to 15 minutes); lower heat to 250°F. and continue to bake until dry and light brown in color (30 to 40 minutes). Remove from paper when slightly cooled. If they stick, put them back in the oven a few minutes longer. Leave the heat on, but open the oven door. Cool. Fill with

Lemon Filling

To **3 egg yolks,** slightly beaten, add **grated rind of 1 lemon** and **1/4 C. lemon juice.** Stir. Add **2/3 C. sugar.** Cook in double boiler until thick. Cool. Fold in **2 C. whipped cream.** Fill nests at least two hours before serving and place uncovered in refrigerator. May be frozen before or after filling. Top with whipped cream before serving. Makes 10 to 12 nests.

PEKING DUST

Li Tzu Kao 栗子糕

Put through a food chopper **2 1/2 lb. chestnuts,** boiled or roasted. Mound on a plate; cover with **1 C. whipped cream;** decorate with **12 glazed walnuts, 12 glazed orange sections,** and **12 glazed cherries,** or other fruit and nuts. Cover with **spun sugar.** Serves 8 to 10.

How to Make Spun Sugar and Glazed Fruit and Nuts

Boil together **2 C. sugar, 1 C. water,** and **2/3 C. white Karo syrup.** Cook to 290° F. Take from fire and spin part of it. To spin the sugar, place two long sticks on a table about 1 1/2 feet apart, extending beyond the table about one foot. Stand on a chair to be at a proper height to spin the sugar. Hold pan in the left hand. Dip the shaker into the syrup and let it drain off slightly. Lift the shaker above the sticks and shake back and forth vigorously with a series of long movements. The sugar will fall in fine strands over the sticks. (To make a shaker, drive about 50 three-inch nails through a four-inch square of wood one inch thick. The nails should be 1/2 inch apart, and the points should extend downward. Add a handle to the top.)

Use the remaining amount of syrup for glazing the fruit and nuts. Dip them individually into the syrup and place on a tray or at once decorate the chestnut mound.

SNOWBALLS

Hsüeh Ch'iu 雪球

This is a Russian dessert that goes particularly well with Chinese food.

Beat **3 egg whites** stiff; gradually add **3 T. powdered sugar,** beating all the time. Heat **2 C. milk;** add **1/4 t. vanilla,** and when milk comes to a boil drop heaping spoonsful of the egg white mixture into the milk. Cover and remove from heat. Let stand 10 minutes. Remove the "snowballs" from milk and use the milk in the

Sauce

Mix **3 T. sugar** with **1 T. cornstarch.** Stir in **2 T. cold milk** and add to the milk in which the "snowballs" were cooked. Bring to a boil and cook until the mixture thickens, stirring constantly. Beat **3 egg yolks.** Pour some of the hot liquid over the egg yolks, stirring constantly. Add egg yolks to remaining hot liquid and cook 1 minute. Flavor with **1 t. vanilla** (and rum, if desired.) Cool and serve with "snowballs" in sherbet glasses. Serves 6.

ORANGE TEA

Chen Tzu Keng 陳子羹

Peel **3 sweet oranges** or tangerines, remove membrane and seeds, break pulp into small pieces; or use 1 can of Mandarin oranges (310 grams) without removing the membranes. In a separate pan mix **1/2 C. sugar, 2 T. cornstarch,** and **2 1/2 C. water** or juice from the can plus water. Boil a few seconds, stirring constantly. Add oranges and simmer a few minutes. Simmer only a few seconds when canned oranges are used. Serve hot. Serves 4 to 6.

Note: Canned pineapple may be used in place of oranges, or a half and half combination.

WALNUT BARS

Ho T'ao Ping 合桃餅

Beat **1 egg** and **1 C. brown sugar** until mixture is very smooth. Stir in **1 C. walnuts**, chopped, 1/2 t. **vanilla,** and **3/4 C. flour** sifted with **1/2 t. soda** and a **pinch of salt.** Spread the batter in a greased pan 7″ × 11″ × 1 1/2″ and bake at 325°F. for about 25 minutes, or until a cake tester comes out clean. Cut the cake into bars or squares while it is still warm. These are good frosted with an uncooked mixture of powdered sugar and water or milk. Makes 12 to 15 bars.

Hurry men at work, not at meat.
催 工 莫 催 食

83

SOUR CREAM PUDDING

Suan Nai Yu Ping 酸奶油餅

Mix **2 C. flour, 3 t. baking powder, 1/2 t. baking soda,** and a **pinch of salt;** add **1 C. sour cream.** Spread batter into 2 greased baking dishes, about 8 inches in diameter and 2 inches deep. Cover batter with **1 1/3 C. brown sugar** and **1 1/3 C. sour cream.** Bake about one half hour at 325°F. Serve warm with coffee cream. May be made in advance and reheated. Serves 10 to 12.

The more you eat, the less flavor; the less you eat, the more flavor.

多吃少滋味少吃多滋味

84

TWO-STEP CAKE

Mi Tsao Ping 密棗餅

Cream **3/4 C. butter** or shortening and **1 C. brown sugar.** Mix **1 1/2 C. flour, 1 1/2 C. rolled oats,** and **1 t. soda;** add to the creamed butter. Spread half of the above mixture into a well-greased pan 8″ × 12″ and spread over it the following

Filling

Boil **1/2 lb. dates,** chopped, **1/2 C. brown sugar,** and **1 C. cold water** until the dates are soft. Cool. Cover this filling with the remaining cake mixture and bake at 325°F. about 30 minutes or until browned. Serve warm with whipped cream. Serves 12 to 15. May be frozen after cooking.

Miscellaneous

CHINESE FRIED RICE

Ch'ao Fan 炒飯

Heat pan, add **2 T. oil,** and fry **2 C. onions,** coarsely chopped, until brown. Add **2 C. cold cooked rice** and sauté. Add a mixture of **2 eggs,** stirred slightly, **1 T. soy sauce,** and **1/2 t. salt;*** sauté until done. For variety add 2 C. chopped cooked meat (bacon, ham, shrimp, left-overs) or green peppers, chopped, or peanuts, shelled and roasted. Heat thoroughly. Serves 4 to 6.

* May be made in advance to this point and fried in a small amount of oil just before serving.

The mouth is an unlimited measure.
口 是 無 量 斗

89

CHINESE SALAD DRESSING

Leng P'en 冷盆

Mix **3 T. vinegar** or lemon juice, **3 T. soy sauce,** and **1 T. sugar.** Add **2 T. salad oil** slowly, stirring constantly.

Use with cucumbers, cabbage, lettuce, tomatoes, or any other vegetable. It is delicious on bits of left-over meat. For an additional flavor, add **1 t. fresh ginger,** chopped, to the salad. For a low-calory diet, the oil may be omitted. The dressing may be made in advance and does not need refrigeration.

Anywhere in the world salt is good to eat; anywhere in the world money is good to use.

吃 盡 天 下 鹽 好 用 盡 天 下 錢 好

EGG NOODLES

Chi Tan Mien 鶏蛋麵

To **1 egg,** slightly beaten, add enough sifted **hard flour** or all-purpose flour to make a stiff dough. Roll out very thin on a well-floured board. Leave to dry slightly. Roll the slightly dried dough like a jelly roll and cut into fine strips. Cook in boiling water about 3 minutes. Drain; rinse with cold water; and drain well. Reheat before serving. Serves 6.

Salt may be added to the water in which the noodles are boiled, or 1/2 t. salt may be added to the dough.

A handy way to reheat noodles is to place a serving in a wire strainer, immerse it in boiling water for a few seconds, take out, shake to drain, and serve.

If you wish to make noodles a week or more in advance, dry them and store in a ventilated container. Do not fry these dried noodles. They should be boiled about 5 minutes.

Fried Noodles

Instead of boiling the fresh noodles, fry them in deep oil until light brown. Fried noodles may be kept for a month or more by storing them in a well-sealed metal or glass container.

HOW TO COOK RICE

Fan 飯

Wash **1 C. rice** in cold water several times until water poured off is clear. Add **1 1/2 C. cold water.** Place in pot and cover. Boil over a hot fire until the water is evaporated. Do not stir while rice is boiling; otherwise rice will not stand out as separate grains. Keep warm until ready to serve, leaving the cover on. If an electric stove is used, heat may be turned off and the covered pot kept on the burner. If it is cooked on a gas stove, turn the flame very low after the water has evaporated.

One cup of uncooked rice makes two cups of cooked rice.

When rice is not well cooked it is because the steam has been unequally distributed.

飯不熟氣不勻

FOODSTUFFS

English	Chinese	Mandarin Romanization
Bamboo Shoots	竹 筍	Chu Sun
Bean Curds	豆 腐	Tou Fu
Bean Sprouts	豆芽菜	Tou Ya Ts'ai
Beef	牛 肉	Niu Jou
Cabbage	白 采	Pai Ts'ai
Cauliflower	菜 花	Ts'ai Hua
Celery	芹 菜	Ch'in Ts'ai
Chestnuts	栗 子	Li Tzu
Chicken	鷄	Chi
Crabs	螃 蟹	P'ang Hsieh
Cucumbers	黃 瓜	Huang Kua
Eggplant	茄 子	Ch'ieh Tze
Fish	魚	Yü
Garlic	蒜	Suan
Ginger	生 薑	Sheng Chiang
Loquat	荔 枝	Li Chih
Lotus Root	藕	Ou
Mushrooms	菌子,香菌, 東茹	Chün Tzu, Hsiang Chün, Tung Ku
Onions	葱	Ts'ung
Pineapple	波 羅	Po Lo
Pork	猪 肉	Chu Jou

Prawns	對 蝦	Tui Hsia
Rice	白 米	Pai Mi
Sesame Oil	胡麻油	Chih Ma Yu
Shrimps	鰕 子	Hsia Tzu
Snow Peas	碗豆莢	Wan Tou Chia
Soy Sauce	醬 油	Chiang Yu
Spinach	菠 菜	Po Ts'ai
String Beans	扁 豆	Pien Tou
Sugar, Brown	紅 糖	Hung T'ang
Water Chestnuts	荸 薺	Pi Ch'i

NOTES

NOTES

NOTES

NOTES

THE ART OF CHINESE COOKING

Visualize a long, narrow room, one end a demonstration kitchen, the other end with chairs for students. At the stove stand two smiling-faced nuns, clad in voluminous white aprons over flowing black robes. Their own obvious enjoyment in their task, as they stir and taste and answer questions, enhances the gay atmosphere, and from the stove exotic odors waft across the room.

These two delightful and courageous American women came to Japan from a war-ravaged China with little else than their skill in Chinese cooking. To earn their living they started to teach, and as their celestial cuisine won fame in the city of Tokyo they could not keep up with the demand. For the benefit of those who were unable to attend their classes, they have written THE ART OF CHINESE COOKING, which describes the tempting variety of Chinese cooking in concise, easy-to-follow style. Here are their secrets. Use them—and good eating !

CHARLES E. TUTTLE COMPANY : PUBLISHERS